The Secret World of Spies

Sally Cowan

The Secret World of Spies

Text: Sally Cowan
Publishers: Tania Mazzeo and Eliza Webb
Series consultant: Amanda Sutera
Hands on Heads Consulting
Editor: Kirstie Innes-Will
Project editor: Annabel Smith
Designer: Leigh Ashforth
Project designer: Danielle Maccarone
Permissions researchers: Lumina Datamatics
Production controller: Renee Tome

Acknowledgements
We would like to thank the following for permission to reproduce copyright material:

Front cover: iStock.com/cyano66; pp. 4, 9, 16: Thomas Pajot/Adobe Stock Photos; p. 4: Only_NewPhoto/Shutterstock.com; p. 5: Gorodenkoff/Shutterstock.com; p. 6: James Thew/Alamy Stock Photo; p. 7 (top): Rawpixel Ltd/Alamy Stock Photo; p. 7 (bottom): Al/Adobe Stock Photos, GK Images/Alamy Stock Photo, Henk Vrieselaar/Alamy Stock Photo, Юлия Данилова/Adobe Stock Photos; pp. 1, 8: Laurence Dutton/E+/Getty Images; p. 9: U.S. Marshals/AP/AAP Photos; p. 9, back cover: iStock.com/elnavegante; p. 10: Dimitrios Karamitros/Alamy Stock Photo; p. 11 (top row): IanDagnall Computing / Alamy Stock Photo, Pictorial Press Ltd/Alamy Stock Photo; (second row): Keystone Press/Alamy Stock Photo, Silver Screen/Flickr; p. 12: J. Wilds/Hulton Archive/Getty Images; p. 13: FRED PROUSER/Reuters; p. 15: MPS Limited, © Cengage Australia; p. 16 (left): Eddie Gerald/Alamy Stock Photo; p. 16 (right): Juliane Thiere/Alamy Stock Photo; p. 17: FlixPix/Alamy Stock Photo; p. 18 (top): sante castignani/Alamy Stock Photo; p. 18 (centre): MONEY SHARMA/AFP/Getty Images; p. 18 (bottom): Stokkete/Shutterstock.com; p. 19 (top): ANGHI/Shutterstock.com; p. 19 (bottom): Trinity Mirror/Alamy Stock Photo; p. 20 (top): WINDCOLORS/Shutterstock.com; p. 20 (bottom): Ermolaev Alexander/Shutterstock.com; p. 21 (top): Science History Images/Alamy Stock Photo; p. 21 (bottom): Michael Vi/Shutterstock.com; p. 22: Nicoleta Ionescu/Shutterstock.com; p. 23: janiecbros/E+/Getty Images; pp. 1, 24: Iordache Elena G/Shutterstock.com; p. 25 (top): Phil/Adobe Stock Photos; p. 25 (bottom): Ed Weiner/Shutterstock.com; p. 26 (left): Maximum Film/Alamy Stock Photo; p. 26 (right): Entertainment Pictures/Alamy Stock Photo; p. 27: Keystone/Hulton Archive/Getty Images; p. 29: Sueddeutsche Zeitung Photo/Alamy Stock Photo; p. 30: Johnny Green - PA Images/PA Images/Getty Images.

Every effort has been made to trace and acknowledge copyright. However, if any infringement has occurred, the publishers tender their apologies and invite the copyright holders to contact them.

NovaStar

ISBN 978 0 17 033520 1

Cengage Learning Australia
Level 5, 80 Dorcas Street
Southbank VIC 3006 Australia
Phone: 1300 790 853
Email: aust.nelsonprimary@cengage.com

For learning solutions, visit **cengage.com.au**

Printed in Malaysia by Papercraft
1 2 3 4 5 6 7 29 28 27 26 25

Nelson acknowledges the Traditional Owners and Custodians of the lands of all First Nations Peoples. We pay respect to Elders past and present, and extend that respect to all First Nations Peoples today.

Contents

A Risky Job

Spies are people who collect secret information about other people or things. This information is called "**intelligence**". Spies are also known as secret agents, because they must do their job in secret: not even their family and friends know that they are spies. Being a spy is risky work. If spies are caught, they can be sent to jail or even face death.

Often, spies work for an **intelligence agency** to keep their country and its citizens safe. These spies work during times of war to help defeat an enemy, but also when there is peace. Spies are found in other areas of life, too, such as in research and business.

In the past, spies recorded conversations in other locations with equipment like this.

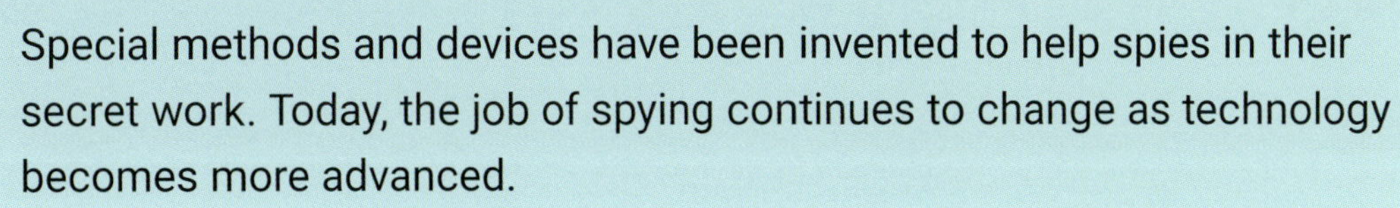

Special methods and devices have been invented to help spies in their secret work. Today, the job of spying continues to change as technology becomes more advanced.

While few people are willing to risk their life being a spy, most are fascinated by the secret world of spying.

The development of new technology has resulted in new ways of spying.

Becoming a Spy

People become spies for different reasons. Some might want to help their country defeat an enemy, especially during a war. They join an intelligence agency. The people in charge of the agency give the spies their jobs, or **missions**. A "handler" at the agency becomes the spy's special contact, through whom all the spy's intelligence is passed. This arrangement minimises the contact that a spy has with people in the agency. That helps keep the spy's identity a secret.

A spy and their handler typically meet in locations where no one will notice them.

Sometimes a person is **recruited** to become a spy because of their job. A person with a government job in a different country is a good candidate for being a spy. They might have access to secret information about that country and its activities. The recruiter can check the background of the candidate to determine whether they might have any concerns about the activities of the foreign government. If so, they might be prepared to become a spy and hand over secret information.

Checking the background of spies is essential, as they need to be loyal to their country.

FAMOUS SPY AGENCIES

Famous spy agencies include:

- MI6 (also called the Secret Intelligence Service) and MI5 (the Security Service) in the United Kingdom (UK)
- the FBI (Federal Bureau of Intelligence) and the CIA (Central Intelligence Agency) in the USA
- the KGB (in English, the Committee for State Security) in the **Soviet Union**; it ended in 1991 after the Soviet Union collapsed
- the FSB (in English, the Federal Security Service) and the SVR (in English, the Foreign Intelligence Service) in Russia.

Types of Spies

SLEEPERS

Many people who decide to be spies do so because they strongly believe in their country or in a particular system of government. Sleeper spies are prepared to wait patiently until the time is right for spying.

So-called "sleepers" are usually sent from their homeland to live and work in a foreign country. They settle into their new home and seek jobs in government departments and security organisations. In these workplaces, they hope to get access to secret intelligence.

Sleeper spies may stay in particular roles for years in the hope of accessing information.

Often, sleepers marry a local person and even have children. They want everyone to think that they are normal members of the community, but their loyalties secretly lie with their homeland. After many years of living a "normal" life, a sleeper can be **activated** by their handler to begin spying.

The Russian Ten

In 2010, a **spy ring** of ten Russian sleepers was unmasked in the USA. Some of the sleepers had been in the country for more than ten years. However, a US spy agency, the FBI, had been closely monitoring all ten, because they had acted in suspicious ways. The Russian sleepers did not provide any valuable intelligence to the Russian government.

The "Russian Ten" was a spy ring of five men and five women sent by the Russian intelligence organisation, the SVR.

SPY SWAP!

Sometimes spy swaps are organised between different countries. Foreign spies who have been caught and held in prison are exchanged. This is what happened with the Russian Ten.

The Cambridge Five

Sleepers can also be recruited to spy on their own homeland for a foreign intelligence agency. One such spy ring was a group of five British university students in the 1930s, who later became known as the Cambridge Five. Although they were British, they believed in **communism**. That was the system of government of the Soviet Union. The students were recruited to spy for the Soviet Union's spy agency, the KGB.

THE SOVIET UNION

The Soviet Union, known as the USSR, was made up of 15 republics that are now these independent countries.

Later, some of these men, including Kim Philby, got important jobs in the British government. For a time, Philby was head of the anti-Soviet section of MI6, Britain's Secret Intelligence Service, while he was spying for the KGB. The Cambridge Five passed top-secret information to the Soviet Union during World War II and afterwards, in the 1950s and 1960s.

The actions of the Cambridge Five were a major intelligence disaster for the UK.

SLEEPERS UNMASKED!

Guy Burgess and Donald Maclean were unmasked in 1951, and Philby in 1963. Blunt and Cairncross kept their secret for decades longer.

MOLES

A spy who **infiltrates** an organisation to pass on its secrets is known as a mole. Kim Philby is one of the most famous moles. A mole can disrupt the plans of the organisation they infiltrate. People in the organisation begin to suspect that someone is giving away intelligence to an enemy. Although suspicions might fall on the mole, spies are trained to be careful not to leave evidence of their activities.

The British press questioned Philby about his involvement with Burgess and Maclean.

MOLE!

Philby was a mole in MI6. In 1951, after Burgess and Maclean were unmasked, suspicions were raised about Philby. He had to leave his job at MI6 but he continued to spy until he **defected** to the Soviet Union in 1963.

DOUBLE AGENTS

Spies can sometimes be "turned" to become double agents. This means a spy working for one agency is persuaded by a rival agency to secretly change their loyalty. This might occur when a spy is discovered. Changing sides can be a way for the spy to avoid being sent to prison.

Sometimes, spies turn when they genuinely come to believe that they are working for the "wrong" side. There are others who turn because they are offered large sums of money to work for the rival agency.

The most famous double agents in Australian history were Soviet couple Vladimir and Evdokia Petrov, who defected to Australia in 1954. Vladimir had failed in his intelligence assignments and feared for his life if he returned to the Soviet Union.

DOUBLE AGENT!

In 2003, Katrina Leung was charged with being a double agent. She worked for the CIA, but was charged with passing information to a Chinese security organisation. The charge was later dismissed due to problems with the evidence.

Katrina Leung

Spy Craft

SPYING SKILLS

Successful spies need certain skills to carry out their risky work. They must be good at observation, which means noticing things in their surroundings, including small details that others might miss. A good memory is also needed: it might be hours before a spy has a chance to write down what they've observed. Sometimes, spies are ordered not to write things down, because it is too risky to have intelligence on their mobile phone, in a note in their pocket or lying around the house.

Quick thinking and problem-solving are also essential skills for spies. They might need to make sudden decisions, for example, if they are following someone or if they are trying to avoid being followed!

Spies also need to be brave, daring and able to avoid showing their true feelings. Keeping up a secret identity means always being alert and able to convince others while working undercover. It can also involve negative things, such as spreading false information and lying to friends and family.

Can you spot ten differences in these two scenes? This activity is similar to a CIA spy recruitment test to determine an applicant's observational skills.
Find the answers on page 32.

MASTERS OF DISGUISE

Spies sometimes need to disguise themselves so that they won't be recognised. Simple disguises might include wigs, glasses, make-up and adding facial hair. More advanced disguises can include incredibly life-like masks. Dental devices can change the look of a person's teeth or the shape of their face, for example, by pushing out their cheeks. Some dental plates can cover the roof of the mouth, which alters the way a person speaks.

Spies might need to walk differently or change their mannerisms when they take on a different identity. They might also speak with a different accent.

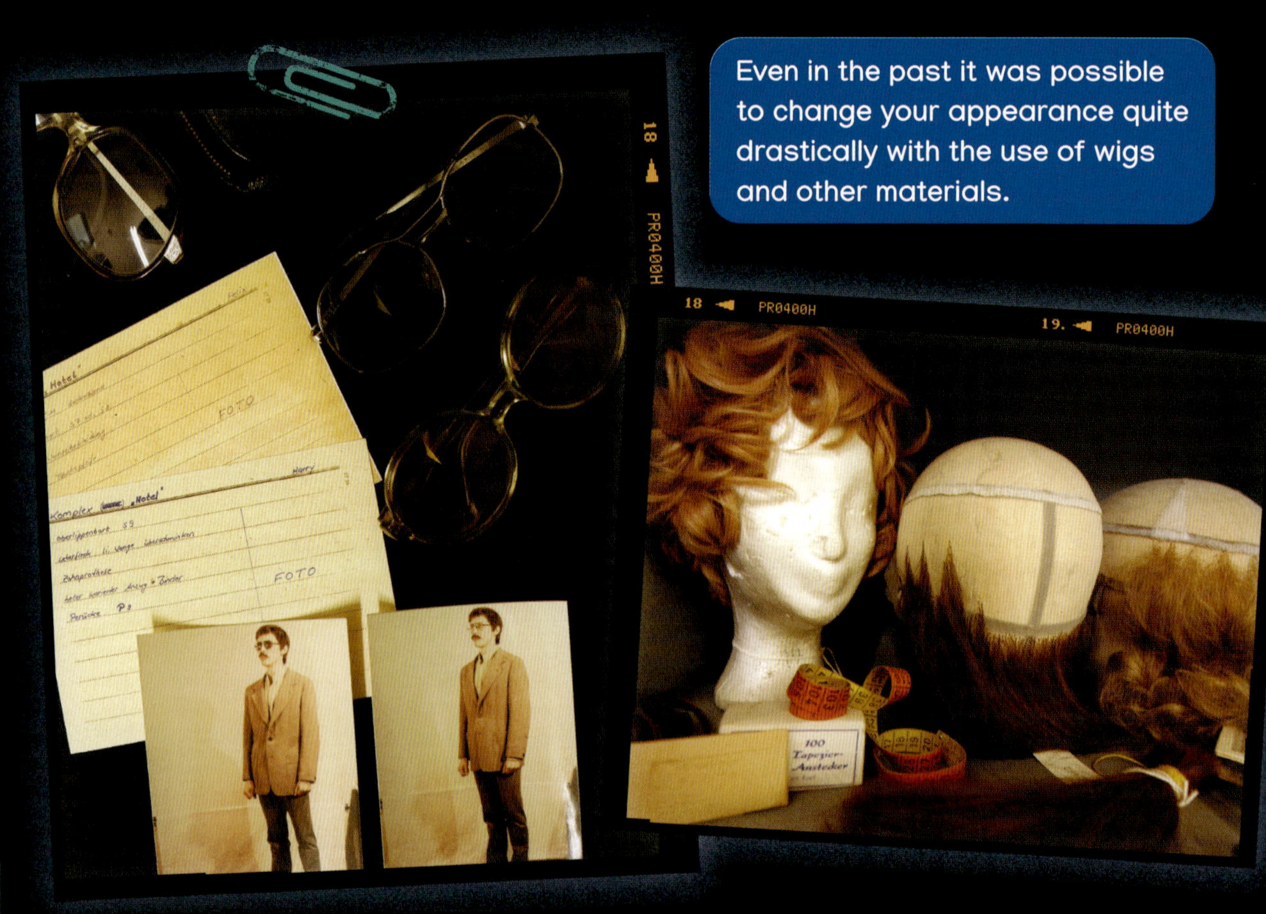

Even in the past it was possible to change your appearance quite drastically with the use of wigs and other materials.

Clothing disguises are also important and need some preparation. If a spy has to do a quick change, for example, if someone is following them along a busy street, they could go from business clothes to casual street clothes in seconds by shedding a few layers. They might unbutton a jacket or shirt and discard them as they walk. Underneath those outer layers, the spy could be wearing a t-shirt or tank top. If they then put on a cap and glasses, carried in their bag, they can completely change their appearance and blend in with the crowd.

By changing clothes, hairstyle and mannerisms, it's possible to appear like a completely different person.

A SPY'S TOOLBOX

Obtaining intelligence quickly and secretly can be a challenge. Some devices, like cameras and microphones, help spies to do this.

For spies in the twentieth century, tiny cameras were invented for photographing secret documents. As technology improved, these cameras could also photograph buildings and large areas. Sometimes the cameras were hidden in everyday items such as pens, bags and clothing. Today, we have high-quality cameras and microphones in mobile phones, but even with this convenient technology, spies might not want to be caught using a phone. So, hidden devices are still used today.

It was less dangerous for a spy to whip one of these small cameras out of a secret pocket than to try to remove documents or use a large camera.

a pen camera

TRENCH COAT TRICKS

The trench coat became a useful garment associated with spies in the twentieth century. It was weatherproof and had many pockets for storing items such as a notebook, weapon, microphone and camera. The coat's drab colour also made its wearer less noticeable, which was useful for a spy in the shadows.

Trench coats like this became so widely associated with spies that they were used in comedy shows about fictitious spies.

Secret listening devices called "bugs" contain hidden microphones. Spies began to use them from the mid-twentieth century. When the bug is secretly placed in a home or office, a spy can eavesdrop on conversations and gather intelligence. Phones can also be bugged, or "tapped", for listening in to phone calls.

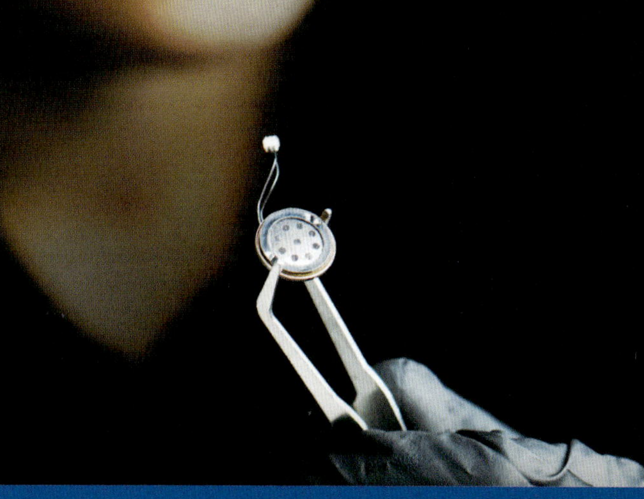

Some tiny bugs have their own battery power and can be attached to an item in a room in seconds.

ACOUSTIC KITTY

In the 1960s, the CIA wired up a cat with a microphone to conduct intelligence field trials. The idea was that the cat, nicknamed Acoustic Kitty, would sit near foreign agents who met in parks and eavesdrop on their conversation without attracting any suspicion. But, like most cats, Acoustic Kitty could not be controlled. It just walked about as it liked, so the idea was abandoned. When this trial was later made public, people called it a form of animal cruelty, but the agency emphasised that the cat wasn't harmed in the process.

CODES AND CODE NAMES

When spies obtain intelligence, it can sometimes be too risky for them to pass it to their handler in person. Furthermore, handlers often work in a different country. So spies have had to develop ways of conveying written intelligence using **codes** and other tricks, such as writing with invisible ink.

Spies and their missions are also given code names. Then, sensitive details don't have to be written in any messages. This helps to keep the spy's identity and mission a secret.

Codes work by replacing letters with other letters or symbols.

CODED PHOTOS?

The Russian Ten spies are believed to have passed on coded intelligence in photos posted to public websites. It has not been explained how they did this.

An image of puppies like this one apparently carried a coded message from the Russian spies.

The Manhattan Project

During World War II, a carefully selected team of American and international scientists were given the mission of developing a top-secret weapon: the atomic bomb. The code name of the mission was the Manhattan Project.

However, one of the scientists, Klaus Fuchs, was a Soviet spy. He succeeded in carrying out what was probably the world's most **consequential** spying mission. Fuchs was code-named "Charles" by the KGB. Another Soviet spy was code-named Mlad, meaning "youngster" in Russian. Fuchs passed on details of the bomb's design to the KGB, enabling the development of atomic bombs in the Soviet Union.

Klaus Fuchs

In 1950, Fuchs confessed to being the Manhattan Project spy. People had their suspicions about who Mlad was, but they have never been proven, which shows how effective that code name was.

LOS ALAMOS

The top-secret work on the Manhattan Project took place in Los Alamos, New Mexico. A secret town had to be built to accommodate all the scientists and some of their families.

Today, tourists can visit the secret town at Los Alamos, which is now a National Historical Park.

High-Tech Spying

In the twenty-first century, spying has become more high-tech, with advances in technology. Spies are also being detected in a wider variety of places, such as universities and in business.

ECONOMIC SPYING

A type of spying called "economic spying" involves stealing research or business secrets. When a lot of money can be made from new methods of production or newly developed products, such as medicines or electronic items, spies will probably be present. These spies might be the researchers in a university or workers in a company.

Modern phones have made it easy to capture copies of documents quickly.

SOFT-DRINK SPY

In 2021, a chemist was sent to prison for 14 years for stealing trade secrets from a large American soft drink company. She had worked as a researcher for the company. The trade secret involved a new technology developed to keep the drink fresh and tasting good in a can without having to use chemicals.

CYBER SPYING

Cyber spying is the use of computers and technology to steal intelligence. Cyber spies can **hack** into the computer systems of governments and businesses. These spies don't have to step out of their home or office to do their job.

TRACKING SATELLITES AND GPS

Satellites orbit Earth in space, continuously taking high-quality images and sending them to spy agencies. The multiple images can provide a detailed three-dimensional view – for example, of the position of a country's weapons installations.

GPS tracking runs on information sent from satellites. Spies use small GPS devices called "trackers". They can be attached to vehicles or put on clothing or in bags. A tracker can allow spies to accurately pinpoint the location of vehicles or people.

Satellites can provide intelligence about another nation's military activities.

SPY SATELLITES

Spy satellites that are high up in space move at about the same speed as Earth's orbit, so they often look over the same area of land. Other spy satellites that orbit closer to Earth move very fast. They can look over more areas of land, but it can be difficult to capture clear images at this speed.

DRONES AND BALLOONS

Drones and balloons are flying devices fitted with cameras and microphones that can be used for spying. Drones can fly fast to follow people during a chase. There are also tiny drones that look like flies and other insects. They contain cameras and microphones for spying and can be flown into rooms.

The expression "being a fly on the wall" is often used when people wish they could eavesdrop on a conversation – but it is now a reality!

Balloons have been used in the past for spying on other countries. Sometimes they are still used today, although satellites have largely taken over. Spy balloons fly at a similar height to passenger planes. An advantage of a balloon over a satellite is that it travels slowly and much closer to the ground, so it can be used to take clear photos.

Spy balloons are used to collect information by flying over other countries.

SPY OR WEATHER BALLOON?

In 2023, a large balloon was detected over the USA. The balloon was suspected of being sent by the Chinese government on a spying mission. It was shot down and examined. Despite the Chinese insisting it was just a weather balloon that had gone off course, the investigators found it could collect secret communication signals that the USA uses for contacting its **allies**.

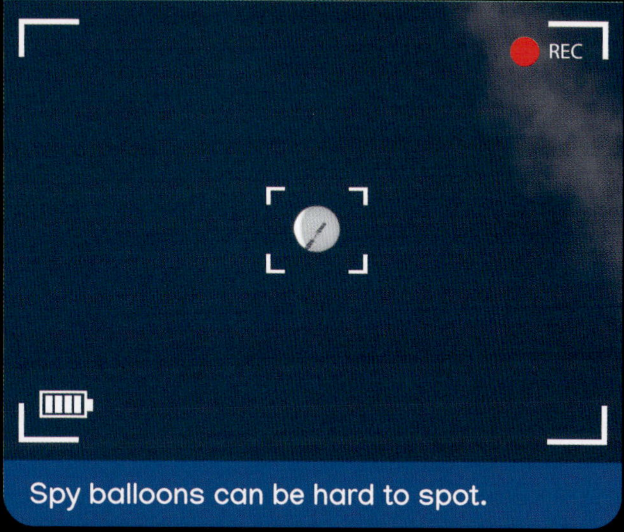

Spy balloons can be hard to spot.

Fascination with Spies

Many people think a spy's job is not only dangerous, but also fascinating and exciting. Thousands of fictional spy stories have been written for children and adults, and there are many films and TV shows. The stories range from realistic to fantasy, but always have lots of action, thrilling stunts and surprising plot twists.

The world of spying is probably so fascinating because it involves a complex mix of **moral dilemmas**. Although spies can help win wars, they might have to spread false information or trick people into trusting them to get intelligence.

Whether we approve of spies or not, they will be around for a long time to come.

Spy movies have entertained people of all ages for many decades.

Nancy Wake: The White Mouse

(1912–2011)

Nancy Wake was a brave and bold spy in World War II. She was awarded the most medals of any woman for her brave actions during the war.

Nancy was born in Aotearoa New Zealand in 1912. Shortly afterwards, her family moved to Sydney, Australia, where she grew up.

At the age of 16, Nancy briefly worked as a nurse, before travelling to New York. There, she became a journalist and loved travelling, seeing new places and meeting people. On a journalistic assignment to Austria, Nancy witnessed the cruel and racist behaviour of the **Nazis** under Adolf Hitler. Throughout the 1930s, she reported on the growing power of the Nazis in Germany and became determined to help defeat them.

Nancy Wake

NAZI GERMANY

The German Nazi Party promoted racist beliefs, blaming the difficult times in Germany after World War I on Jewish people. The Nazis came to power in 1933. Hitler started World War II in 1939 to get more land for Germans and spread Nazi ideas.

In 1939, Nancy married a Frenchman, Henri Fiocca, and moved to the south of France. In 1940, when France was invaded by Germany and put under German rule, Nancy and Henri joined the French **Resistance**. For three years, Nancy worked undercover, helping to disrupt the Germans' communications and transport, and rescuing British and French soldiers and Jewish refugees. She also sent coded messages to England to assist the Allies.

The German secret police, the Gestapo, knew of Nancy's activities and tried to catch her many times. They code-named her the White Mouse, likening her to a pest that was hard to catch. They even offered a large reward for turning her in. In 1943, Nancy fled to England as the Gestapo were closing in on her. In England, she trained as a spy in the top-secret Special Operations Executive. Then in 1944, Nancy parachuted into France with the English code name "Helene".

One of Nancy's most incredible feats occurred after secret radio codes were lost. She volunteered to ride a bicycle 400 kilometres through the French countryside to set up new codes. She believed she could pose as a French housewife returning to her village. Nancy's physical strength, poise and confidence helped her to pass through Nazi checkpoints without raising any suspicions. The White Mouse remained undetected.

Many French people rode bicycles, so Nancy would have looked like one of them as she rode across the countryside.

By the time the Allies freed France in August 1944, Nancy had helped the Resistance obtain weapons, destroy bridges, and even attack a Gestapo base. Only after the victory did Nancy find out that Henri had been tortured and killed by the Gestapo.

Nancy spent the rest of her life moving between the UK and Australia. In Australia, few people knew about her courageous role as a spy in World War II, but in 2004 she was finally awarded the Order of Australia by the government.

In 2011, Nancy died at the age of 98. She had inspired many people to believe in their convictions and never give up in the face of difficulties.

Nancy Wake received the Order of Australia medal for her bravery.

Glossary

activated (*verb*)	put to work, or woken up
allies (*noun*)	other countries that are friends with a country
codes (*noun*)	forms of communication used to keep messages secret, such as using symbols instead of letters
communism (*noun*)	a system of government in which people don't own land or businesses; the government owns and runs these things and is supposed to share wealth evenly
consequential (*adjective*)	having significant and important outcomes
defected (*verb*)	left a country to live in another country with a different system of government
GPS (*noun*)	Global Positioning System; a location system using satellite information
hack (*verb*)	to gain access to a computer system illegally
infiltrates (*verb*)	enters secretly
intelligence (*noun*)	in the world of spying, information that is usually secret and hard to obtain
intelligence agency (*noun*)	a government department that deals with spies and spying
missions (*noun*)	specific tasks that lead to an outcome
moral dilemmas (*noun*)	situations that involve weighing up what the right thing to do is
Nazis (*noun*)	members of the political party that held power in Germany between 1933 and 1945, under Adolf Hitler
recruited (*verb*)	persuaded or hired to do something
Resistance (*noun*)	a secret movement of ordinary citizens who fought against the Nazis in World War II
Soviet Union (*noun*)	a collection of communist countries controlled by Russia; founded in 1922, but ending in 1991 when the member states separated
spy ring (*noun*)	a group of spies working together

Index

Answers

cap; different-coloured car; person in doorway; number of parked cars; balcony; violin case; lights on/off; flower stall; person walking; umbrellas